THE HERB BASKET

Rosemary

Rue & Rose

THE HERB BASKET

Rosemary

Rue & Rose

PHOTOGRAPHY BY GLORIA NICOL

Text by Hazel Evans

JG PRESS

THE HERB BASKET
Rosemary, Rue, and Rose

Designed and created by
THE BRIDGEWATER BOOK COMPANY LTD.

Written by Hazel Evans
Photography by Gloria Nicol

Designer: Jane Lanaway
Project editors: Veronica Sperling/Christine McFadden
Page makeup: Chris Lanaway
Step illustrations: Vana Haggerty
Border illustration: Pauline Allen
Cover: Annie Moss
American adaptation: Josephine Bacon

CLB 4500
© 1996 COLOUR LIBRARY BOOKS LTD
Published in the USA 1996 by JG Press
Distributed by World Publications, Inc.

The JG Press imprint is a trademark of
JG Press, Inc. 455 Somerset Avenue,
North Dighton, MA 02764
All rights reserved.
Color separation by Tien Wah Press
Printed and bound in Singapore by Tien Wah Press

ISBN 1-57215-111-0

CONTENTS

THE JOY OF HERBS 10

INTRODUCING ROSEMARY 13

INTRODUCING RUE 16

INTRODUCING THE ROSE 18

PLANT CARE 20

HARVESTING 22

PRESERVING 24

DISPLAYING YOUR HERBS 26

PLANTING AN HERBAL HEDGE 29

MAKING THE MOST OF RUE 30

DISPLAYING ROSES 31

CHICKEN SOUP WITH ROSEMARY 32

SCRAMBLED EGGS WITH RUE 33

ROAST LAMB AND ROSEMARY 36

ROSE PETAL SORBET AND SYLLABUB 36

ROSE PETAL LIQUEUR 38

ROSE HIP GIN 39

ROSE PETAL JAM 40

ROSE HIP CHUTNEY 41

SCENTED PILLOWS 43

TOILET WATERS 44

COSMETIC CREAMS 46

SOUPS 48

A DRIED ROSEMARY TREE 50

ROSE POTPOURRI 53

HERB CANDLES 54

A NEEDLE KEEPER 56

A ROSE-SCENTED QUILT 59

INDEX 60

ROSEMARY, RUE, AND ROSE

THE JOY OF HERBS

Rosemary

Rue

Rose

ERBS HAVE BEEN important in our lives ever since man first walked the earth. Used for food and especially for medicine they decorate our gardens too, adding color and interest, and often perfume as well.

Herbs have always been associated with myth and magic, perhaps because of the mystery surrounding the medicines that were made from them. In ancient Egypt, herbalists kept their skills secret and carried a magic cask of medicines and a magician's rod. Before treatment could begin, the gods had to be called on to cast out the devil, because it was thought that sickness was a manifestation of evil spirits.

In medieval times, the monks became the herbalists in Europe, though knowledge and skill at using herbs as remedies was not confined to clerics. The lay herbalists were often elderly women whose herbal lore was at times mistaken for witchcraft.

Herbs have had many strange properties attributed to them over the years. In the 16th century, the Doctrine of Signatures dominated medicine. According to the Doctrine, a plant resembles the part of the body that it can cure. Lungwort, for instance, has blotchy markings on its leaves which were thought to look like diseased lungs, and infusions of the plant were used to treat lung disorders. Strangely enough, lungwort happens to be an effective cough medication, and is still used widely by herbalists for lung complaints.

In modern times, as we become more uneasy about powerful drugs, many people are returning to herbal medicine. We are also rediscovering the delights of herbs to liven up jaded palates, giving a sharper more interesting taste to everyday foods.

Find out for yourself how a sprig or two of rosemary improves roast lamb – be adventurous, add a trace of rue to an omelet, or rose petals to a dessert. The world of herbs awaits you!

ROSEMARY, RUE, AND ROSE

Rosemary makes a handsome mature shrub even when grown in pots.

INTRODUCING ROSEMARY

ROSEMARY IS THE herb of remembrance. It is the herb of fidelity, and was placed on the graves of the dead to pledge eternal faithfulness. Rosemary is similarly linked with love and romance. The Romans used it as an aphrodisiac, and young maidens in medieval times slipped a sprig under their pillows so their true love would come to them in their dreams. Rosemary was added to the loving-cup passed round at a wedding, and the bride would give her new husband a sprig of rosemary to hold to ensure he remained faithful to her.

It has been famous throughout history and valued for many reasons – it was used to make wine, medicine and scent as well as an aromatic in the kitchen. It is said that a rosemary bush sheltered the Virgin Mary on her flight into Egypt, and that when she spread her cloak over a rosemary, the white flowers turned blue. And today in many villages in the Mediterranean region, linen is spread over rosemary bushes to dry and perfume them at the same time. It is also said that rosemary will survive for 33 years, the length of Christ's life.

The ill-fated Anne of Cleves wore rosemary in her crown on her marriage to Henry V111.

ABOVE *Rosemary can be used to make attractive wreaths.*

These properties are immortalized in Shakespeare's "Hamlet" in Ophelia's famous lines:

"There's rosemary, that's for remembrance; pray love, remember…"

Rosemary was also Napoleon's favorite perfume – he used more than a hundred bottles of rosemary water during his honeymoon alone.

This aromatic, woody shrub comes from the Mediterranean where it can be found everywhere; perfuming the hillsides of Provence, growing in the ruins of temples in Greece. The word "rosemary" comes from the Latin *ros maris*, "dew of the sea," and in Italy it still grows abundantly along the coastline.

Rosemary was employed extensively by the Romans who used it to preserve food and as medication. The plant is a valuable antiseptic and has insect-repellant properties. In Europe in the Middle Ages, linen chests were made from rosemary wood to deter moths. It was also thought to protect against the Plague, and was carried in little leather pouches and inhaled while walking through a plague-ridden area, as well as tossed on the fire to purify the air. It was burned, too, in the chambers of judges who feared catching jail-fever from the prisoners they tried. The pungent flavor gave it great culinary importance in medieval times as a way of disguising the unpleasant taste of rancid meats. Today it is used mainly to partner and perfume lamb.

Culpeper says that rosemary "clears dim sight and taketh away spots, marks, and scars on the skin." Gerard, another herbalist, was more down-to-earth about its properties: "The distilled water of the floures of rosemary being drunke at morning and evening first and late, taketh away the stench of the mouth and breath and make it very sweet."

Rosemary is a traditional ingredient in cosmetics, hair rinses, and perfumes, and was thought at one time to prevent baldness. Benche's herbal, dated 1525, says: "Smell of it

ABOVE *Seek out decent-sized bunches of fresh herbs from good greengrocers.*

oft and it shall keep thee youngly."

It is said that where rosemary grows "Missis is master." Students in ancient Greece twined rosemary around their heads to stimulate the memory while studying. An infusion of rosemary was taken in the 17th century to prevent forgetfulness, and recent research has found that the scent of its volatile oil really does stimulate the brain.

14

ROSEMARY, RUE, AND ROSE

"BENENDEN BLUE" *has dark-blue flowers, and there are white ("Alba") and pink ("Roseus") varieties too.*

"MAJORCAN PINK" *has clear, blue flowers and bright, green leaves. It is only half-hardy.*

ABOVE *Half-hardy rosemary grown in pots can be brought indoors in Winter.*

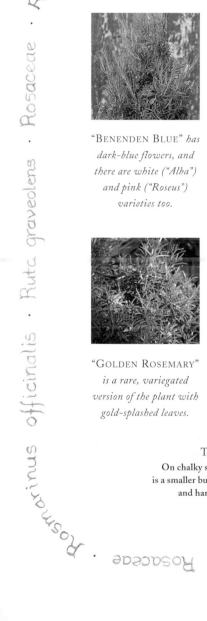

"GOLDEN ROSEMARY" *is a rare, variegated version of the plant with gold-splashed leaves.*

"WHITE ROSEMARY" *is hardy and has white flowers with faint blue veining in them.*

TIP
On chalky soil, rosemary is a smaller but more fragrant and hardy plant.

"MISS JESSOP'S UPRIGHT"
This is the best rosemary for hedging.

ROSMARINUS OFFICINALIS REPENS
If you want something for ground-cover, choose this prostrate rosemary.

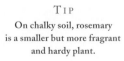

INTRODUCING RUE

RUE IS KNOWN as "the herb of grace," and it certainly makes a graceful sight in any garden with its deeply indented, blue-green leaves. It grows wild on the hillsides around the Mediterranean. Rue is a woody plant with attractive tiny, green-yellow flowers which appear in midsummer. Of the cultivated varieties, "Jackman's Blue" has dark, metallic-looking leaves, while the variegated version (*Ruta graveolens* "Variegata") is tipped with cream. Kept well-clipped, rue makes an unusual hedge around a herb garden.

Rue's strong and distinctive bitter flavor is used in after-dinner drinks such as *grappa,* the Italian brandy, and was mixed with honey to make sack, a type of mead drunk in Shakespeare's time. It was also much prized by the Greeks as one of the components of mithridate, an antidote to poisons.

The herb is said to ward off the evil effects of witchcraft and magic, and was carried in the Middle Ages as a protection from the Plague. One of the ingredients of the once famous "Four Thieves Vinegar" which protected grave-robbers, it was also thought to have supernatural powers and to grant the power of second sight.

RIGHT *A budding rue plant will develop glorious yellow flowers.*

Around the house, rue makes a useful insect repellent. It is used widely in herbal and homeopathic medicine to heal menstrual problems, rheumatism, and high blood pressure, but its toxic properties mean that if large quantities are required it must be taken under medical supervision. When you garden with rue, be sure to wash the sap off your skin, as it can cause an allergic reaction that brings blisters especially in strong sunlight.

ABOVE *Rue goes well with brightly colored flowers in a bouquet.*

Many people believed rue improved the eyesight, and both Michelangelo and Leonardo da Vinci are said to have used infusions of it to aid their inner

INTRODUCING THE ROSE

THE ROSE HAS been called the "Queen of Flowers" and it has certainly reigned in gardens all over the world longer than any other flower. Fossilized roses more than 35 million years old have been found, and it appears in a fresco painted at Knossos in Greece dating back to 1500 BC. In ancient Persia, at the wedding feasts of the Mogul Emperors, the bride was carried in a boat along a canal filled with rosewater.

Cleopatra is said to have entertained Mark Anthony on a carpet of rose petals in ancient Egypt, and Achilles used roses to decorate his shield. But it was the Romans who used roses with everything, and especially at banquets, because they believed the petals were a protection against drunkenness. At a rather boisterous party, a certain nobleman, Heliogabalus, showered his guests with so many rose petals that he accidentally suffocated seven of them. At Nero's banquets, food was sprinkled with petals and guests were sprayed with rose water. His floors were lined with a thick layer of petals, and doves with rose-perfumed wings flew overhead. The rose has also been used as an emblem in battle, notably the White Rose of York and the Red Rose of Lancaster in the War of the Roses (1455.)

Featured since the beginning of time in cookery and in medicine, the rose is used above all for perfume in which it is the most important ingredient. It takes 250 pounds of petals to produce just one ounce of essential oil.

ABOVE *The sensual beauty of roses is a source of endless pleasure.*

A bottle of Joy, the fragrance by Jean Patou, one of the most expensive fragrances in the world, contains the essence of almost six hundred roses.

Many families of roses are grown for their fragrance, notably centifolias which have large pink cabbage-like flowers said to contain a hundred petals. Another fragrant favorite is the damask rose, so-called because it came originally from Damascus. It was also grown at Pompeii, and produces highly-scented, soft pink ruffled blooms.

The favorite roses for a herb garden today are the gallicas, *rosa gallica officinalis*, the apothecary's rose, with its deep red petals and *rosa gallica* "versicolor," and "rosamundi" with its distinctive striped blooms.

BELOW *Try massing roses together tightly in a container for maximum effect. You don't always need foliage in a flower decoration.*

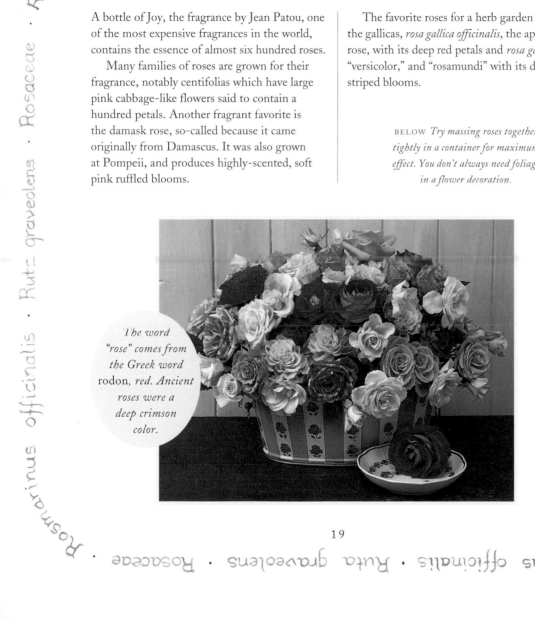

The word "rose" comes from the Greek word rodon, *red. Ancient roses were a deep crimson color.*

PLANT CARE

ROSEMARY
Rosmarinus officinalis

Rosemary is an evergreen perennial shrub which grows up to 3 feet high and prefers a sunny, sheltered spot. It needs a well-drained soil and, once full-grown, dislikes being moved.

Rosemary is very much an all-purpose plant. You can start it from seed undercover, in a seed-tray, or in pots but it prefers some bottom heat. Take cuttings from non-flowering shoots in midsummer or late Summer. If your winters are harsh, overwinter the plant in a cold frame. You can also root sprigs in Spring by suspending them in a glass of water. Rosemary can also be layered. Simply peg down a low-growing branch, making a small cut in the underside of the stem, and cover with soil. Anchor it with a hoop made from a small piece of wire or a large hairpin.

Set rosemary cuttings out in a tray of soil in late summer. In harsh Winters, keep in a cold frame or cold greenhouse. Cuttings should have rooted by the Spring.

RUE
Ruta graveolens

This hardy perennial grows to a height of 2 feet and likes a sunny spot. It does best in thin or poor soil.

Rue can be grown from seed which should be mixed with a little sand when sowing as the seeds are so fine. The hybrid "Jackman's Blue," however, should be started from softwood cuttings taken in early Summer.

Cut mature plants back in the Spring to stop them from becoming spindly and again in mid-summer after flowering. Divide large plants when necessary. Protect variegated rue from hard frosts in Winter.

20

THE ROSE
Rosa

Plant roses any time from Fall through early Spring. Roses are "greedy feeders" so dig in plenty of manure around them. If your rose is bare-rooted, make a little mound beneath the base of the plant, then spread out the roots like the spokes of an umbrella. If your rose has been grafted onto a rootstock (look for the scar on the stem) make sure the graft is just above soil level.

Shake the plant gently from time to time as you fill in the soil around it. Tread the topsoil firmly with your feet to anchor the rose in place.

1. *Plant roses on a dry day when there is no cold, prevailing wind. If the day is too cold, store the plant in a bucket of water under cover for later planting. Dig a hole wide enough to take the plant comfortably.*

2. *Make a little mound of soil in the hole, where the base of the plant is to go. Then put the plant in place, spreading its roots out as you go.*

3. *Scatter a little bone-meal around the roots then fill with soil. Check that the scar on the stem is above ground level if the rose is grafted.*

4. *Shake the plant from time to time as you fill in the soil, to make sure no air pockets are left around the roots. Tamp down the soil around the bush.*

HARVESTING

RAGRANT Rosemary, Rue, and Rose have many uses from potpourri to desserts. Use them fresh if you can, but dry some to use during the Winter months.

HARVESTING ROSEMARY

You can harvest rosemary all year round. Flowering shoots should be picked in the middle of the day, after the dew has disappeared off the blooms. Pick the top fourth only of full-grown plants for the best results in cooking or drying. The best quality of all is cut from the plant before it has flowered.

> **TIP**
> To retain maximum potency, store your dried herbs in sealed jars kept in a dark place, rather than a paper bag.

HARVESTING RUE

If you want to dry rue, cut back the top half of the plant in Spring and again after it has flowered. The flowering sprigs can also be cut to use in flower decoration or to dry. Wear rubber gloves, or wash your hands immediately after handling rue, as the sap can blister the skin.

HARVESTING ROSES

Always use pruning-shears when harvesting roses. Pick buds for drying when they are still tight-packed, or just before they open if you are using them as cut flowers.

If you are picking rose petals for food, make sure that you take them from plants that have not been sprayed with herbicide or insecticide. Petals for potpourri should be harvested just as the flowers are beginning to look blousy and overblown.

If the stems are hard and woody, hammer the ends gently or make a 1-inch vertical cut up the base of each stem and discard any foliage that will end up under water. Then put the roses in a bowl of tepid water and make a slanting cut across the bottom tips of the stems again, under water. This eliminates any air bubbles that may have formed in the stems when they were first cut.

Leave rosehips on the bushes as long as possible before picking them, so that they have time to mature.

ABOVE *A bowl of fallen petals makes an attractive display for the table.*

PRESERVING

DRYING ROSEMARY

Simply hang branches of rosemary upside down in a warm place away from direct light to dry. The faster the drying process, the more volatile oils will be left in the leaves. The flowers will be the first to dry, and can be shaken from the branch into a separate container after a day or so.

DRYING RUE

Rue tends to lose its attractive bluish hue if it is dried in the light, so keep it in as dark a place as possible. Pick individual stems and lay them on sheets of newspaper on racks. Then they can be crumbled and put into jars and used to make insect-repellent sachets or put out in bowls for the same purpose.

Branches of rue for dried flower decoration are best dried by simply standing them in a jar without water.

Rue makes a very attractive pressed plant to decorate lampshades, cards, and candles. Choose small shoots: arrange them carefully on sheets of paper and cover with absorbent kitchen paper. Use a flower-press or sandwich them between heavy books.

ABOVE *Sprigs of rue look very attractive when pressed. Place them between sheets of absorbent paper before pressing in a flower-press.*

ABOVE *Dried rue gives an attractive musky scent to potpourri. Dry it on racks, then crumble it.*

ABOVE *Long-stemmed
dried rosebuds make a delightful,
lasting gift.*

DRYING ROSES

Rosebuds and roses should be hung upside
down to dry in bunches, away from the light
but in an airy place. Alternatively, they dry
particularly well in silica gel, keeping both their
color and their shape.

DRYING ROSE PETALS

Gather your petals when the dew has dried off
in the sun. Spread them immediately on sheets
of absorbent kitchen paper or newspaper, pulling
the petals off separately and making sure they
do not touch each other.

If you are going to use them for a potpourri,
sprinkle with some of the spices you are going
to use (eg, powdered clove or cinnamon) to
discourage ants or any small insects that may
otherwise settle on them.

Alternatively, lay out the petals on paper on
trays or in a colander and put them in an oven at
the lowest setting, leaving the door slightly ajar.
Drying will take up to two or three days.

DRYING ROSEHIPS

Rosehips should be spread out on sheets of paper
on racks to dry. Make sure they do not touch
each other.

DISPLAYING YOUR HERBS

ROSEMARY and roses, set off by the blue-gray foliage of rue, deserve a prime place in any flower plot. Not all of us have gardens or yards, but even if you don't have any growing space outdoors, you can always train some rosemary into indoor topiary in a pot, or grow colorful miniature roses with rue on a sunny windowsill. Take bunches of fresh herbs when visiting, instead of the traditional cut-flower bouquet. They'll be much appreciated.

A ROSEMARY RING

ROSEMARY, with its fine, needle-like leaves like pine-needles, makes an ideal candidate for potted topiary. Whether you keep your plant indoors or outdoors it is possible to train it in many different ways. Here are the instructions for making a rosemary ring, but you could twist the wire into any other shape that appeals to you.

TIP
Rosemary looks equally good growing over shapes other than a ring. Try turning it into a tiny triangular tree, for instance, or a square.

MATERIALS
pliers
thin wire coathanger
suitable pot
potting mixture
1 large rosemary plant or
2 large rooted rosemary cuttings
twine or twist ties

1. Using the pliers, straighten the coat hanger and then bend the center into a circle about 10 inches in diameter, or any other convenient size.

2. Bend the ends at right angles and twist together to make a straight stem. Now bend both pieces out and around to form a circular base to fit in the pot. Sit the hoop in place.

3. *Half-fill the pot with good quality soil mixture. Plant the rosemary at the base of the hoop and twist the plant's stems around the wire, fastening it with twine or twist ties. Or plant the two cuttings at the base and tie each one around one side of the circle.*

RIGHT *Keep a large bunch of rosemary to hand in the kitchen. It will inspire your cooking.*

ABOVE *A garden path lined with rosemary bushes will produce a delicious fragrance as you brush against it.*

PLANTING AN HERBAL HEDGE

AROMATIC HEDGES made from herbs make a perfect fragrant edging to a narrow path. Rosemary is great for this purpose as it grows vigorously and soon thickens up to make a dense border which is easily maintained.

A rosemary hedge can be clipped to a strict shape or left to flower to provide extra color.

If you have time to spare, you can plant a rosemary hedge by taking cuttings in the Fall and setting them straight into the ground. Put in twice as many as you need, in the hope that half of them will survive the winter and "take." Or you can buy container-grown plants for a speedy start.

Either way, use a length of twine to work out a straight line. Dig a row of planting holes and plant your hedge in the Spring to give it a chance to get well established throughout the summer before the cold weather comes. Trim the tips once a year to encourage it to bush out.

Finish off your hedge by making rosemary standards: find a good straight plant with a single stem. Plant it in place, tie it to a bamboo stake, and encourage it to grow onward and upward by removing lower side-shoots. Once the rosemary has reached the required height, continue to remove side-shoots off the stem but allow the top to bush out, pinching out the tips of shoots to make a rounded ball shape.

1. Use twine or tightly stretched rope to mark out the site of your hedge, then fork the site over thoroughly and add some fertilizer to give your rosemary cuttings a flying start.

2. Using a purpose-cut piece of stick as a measure, set your rosemary cuttings out at intervals, putting in twice as many as you need, in case some of them fail to take.

29

ROSEMARY, RUE, AND ROSE

MAKING THE MOST OF RUE

TIP
Rue grows to a medium height and likes sun, so mix it with other plants in the center rather than the back of a flowerbed, where its splendid leaves will be shown off to good effect.

LEFT *The attractive leaves of rue mix well with other herbs.*

RUE'S GOOD-LOOKING blue-green leaves mix well with many other plants. Try it in a windowbox with tulips and other bright bulbs, or surrounding bulbs in a tub.

Rue makes a perfect foil for miniature roses, especially pink ones. It also looks good with lavender, toning in with its silver-gray leaves and emphasizing the purple-blue color of the flowers. Contrast its foliage, too, with sharp yellow tones - of golden marjoram for instance.

Clipped back well every Spring, rue becomes shrubby and dense and makes a good edging for a small herb garden where larger plants would look out of scale.

Try growing rue, too, in garden urns, partnered with forget-me-nots which intensify its unusual coloring.

Variegated rue, its leaves splashed with cream, looks good planted with daffodils, tulips, and other Spring flowers.

30

DISPLAYING ROSES

TIP
Miniature roses now come in climbing and standard, as well as conventional varieties. Grow them in pots but remember they are basically outdoor plants and should only be brought indoors to flower.

RIGHT *Small roses grow well alongside herbs in a windowbox*

T HERE ARE so many ways of displaying the many members of the rose family. Plant old-fashioned shrub roses either side of a pathway to make a fragrant walk. Train hardy rambling roses over a frame to make a rose bower in a corner of the garden. Use climbers round the door, partnered by clematis or honeysuckle. Large-flowered roses (formerly known as hybrid tea-roses) are best confined to a bed of their own. But underplant them with something to complement their good looks and cover their bare stems – lavender or rosemary for instance. Standard roses look best in a formal garden – you could use one as the centerpiece of a herb plot. Don't forget you can buy ground-cover roses too, to scramble over a slope, and the rugosa roses make a wonderful flowering hedge. Not all roses are scented, so choose carefully. Most of the perfumed roses are red, the deeper the color the heavier the fragrance.

31

CHICKEN SOUP WITH ROSEMARY

DELICIOUS LEFTOVERS

Leftovers from a roast chicken can be used to make this delicious and unusual soup.

INGREDIENTS

Serves 4

2 carrots

2 onions

1 chicken carcass

2 tsp dried rosemary leaves

juice of ½ lemon

sour cream

❖ Clean and chop the carrots, and peel and chop the onions. Put in a saucepan with the chicken carcass, and add enough water to cover. Cover the pan and simmer until any meat attached to the carcass is softened and floats free.

❖ Strain off the liquid, cool it, then skim off the fat (the easiest way to do this is to first leave the liquid in the refrigerator overnight).

❖ Drop the rosemary leaves into the skimmed liquid, add the lemon juice, reheat, and serve with a swirl of sour cream.

SCRAMBLED EGGS WITH RUE

TIP
Used very sparingly, rue can give an intriguing, slightly bitter taste to egg and cheese dishes. Try adding two or three pieces of chopped leaf to an omelette or add some to a cheese sauce.

INGREDIENTS

Serves 2
4 large eggs
4 tbs butter
¹/₂ tsp minced rue
1 tbs heavy cream
2 slices lox (optional)

❖ Beat the eggs and season them with salt and pepper. Using a small, nonstick saucepan, heat half the butter until it begins to foam, swirling it around the bottom of the pan. Pour in the eggs and stir vigorously with a fork, scooping the egg away from the sides.

❖ Take the pan off the heat while the egg is still liquid, stir in the chopped rue, the rest of the butter, and the cream. Serve immediately with slivers of lox, if liked.

33

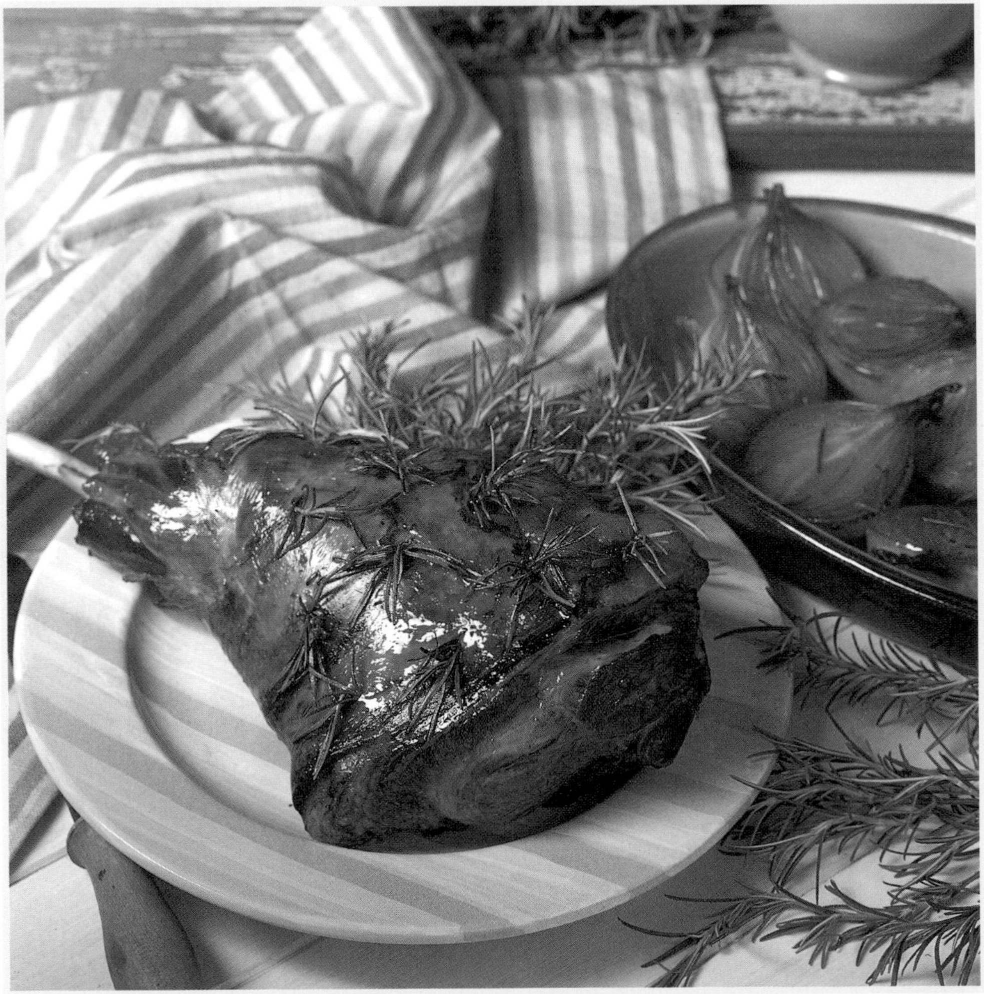

ROAST LAMB AND ROSEMARY

LAMB AND rosemary make a perfect partnership, for the herb not only perfumes the meat but counteracts its tendency toward greasiness.

MAKE NEAT pockets in a leg or shoulder of lamb and tuck sprigs of rosemary inside. Or cut slits in the skin and poke single leaves in place, or strew the leaves on top. Baste the joint well with the pan juices as it cooks, then use the fat as a basis of a rich, rosemary-flavored gravy.

Use rosemary, too, on the barbecue: burn little bundles of it among the charcoal, or lay lamb chops to broil on rosemary sprigs over a fire. Wrap Cornish rock game hens in kitchen foil with rosemary and other herbs , and slow-cook in a barbecue pit or smoker.

CARAMEL ONIONS WITH ROSEMARY

INGREDIENTS

Serves 4

4 large onions
4 tsp softened butter
4 tsp brown sugar
1 tbs rosemary leaves

TIP

Make your own caramelized onion preserve or "jam" to serve with meats. Cook onion slices with brown sugar, a little butter, a dash of sherry, and a little dried rosemary. Bottle and store.

❖ Peel the onions, and cut a thin slice off the top of each so you have a flat surface. Cook the onions whole, in boiling salted water, for about 20 minutes, then remove and drain.

❖ Pound the butter with the sugar. Arrange the onions close together in an ovenproof dish and spread the flat tops with the butter/sugar mix. Sprinkle with the rosemary leaves.

❖ Bake in a preheated oven at 400 degrees for about 30 minutes, until the onions are cooked and golden-brown.

❖ Alternatively, arrange the onions around a roast in the roasting-pan.

ROSE PETAL SORBET

T HE DELICATE perfume of the rose is delicious in desserts. Try adding it to your favorite recipe for homemade ice cream, or use it in a sweet soufflé. Never take petals from bushes that have been sprayed with chemicals.

INGREDIENTS

Serves 4

½ cup superfine sugar
2 cups water
grated rind and juice of 2 lemons
¾ pound scented rose petals
2 tsps rosewater
1 egg white

❖ Put the sugar, water, and grated lemon rind in a saucepan. Boil briskly, stirring, until the sugar has completely dissolved, then simmer for 6 minutes.

❖ Remove from the heat, add the rose petals, and cool. Strain into a bowl, and add the lemon juice and rosewater. Pour into a shallow icetray to freeze for 2 hours or until mushy.

❖ Decant the mixture into a bowl. Stiffly whisk the egg white and fold it in.

❖ Return the mixture to the freezer and re-freeze completely. Serve in scoops in sundae glasses.

ROSE PETAL SYLLABUB

INGREDIENTS

Serves 4

a handful of scented rose petals
⅔ cup medium sweet white wine
1¼ cups heavy cream
juice of ½ lemon
2 egg whites
½ cup rose-scented sugar

❖ Infuse the rose petals overnight in the wine, then drain off the wine and reserve. Whip the cream and mix with the wine and lemon juice in a bowl. Whisk the egg whites stiffly and fold in the sugar, then fold into the wine mixture.

❖ Pour the mixture into sundae glasses and chill well. Serve decorated with rose petals.

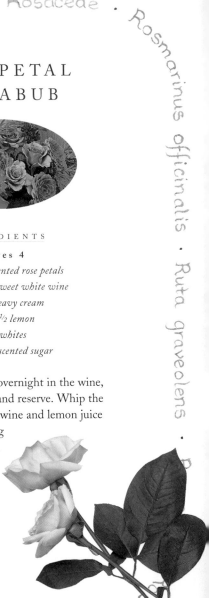

ROSE PETAL LIQUEUR

ERB AND flower liqueurs are delightful
to serve either before or after a meal.
If you prefer you can substitute vodka
or rum for the brandy.

INGREDIENTS

Makes 1 bottle
3 cups rose petals
strip of lemon rind
1 bottle brandy
1½ cups sugar

❖ Choose roses that have not been sprayed with
insecticides or polluted by exhaust fumes. Rinse
and carefully dry the petals if they are dusty.
❖ Put the rose petals and the lemon rind in a
wide-mouthed screwtop jar.
❖ Cover with the brandy, seal, and leave in a
cool place for 28 days, shaking occasionally.
❖ Add the sugar, and leave for 14 days, shaking
well once or twice a day, so that the
sugar is dissolved.
❖ Strain off the petals and
discard them. Decant the brandy
into a sterilized bottle. Seal
tightly and leave to mature for at
least a month in a cool, dark place
before using.

ROSEHIP GIN

HIS IS A variation on the old-fashioned sloe gin of our grandmother's time. If you make it in the Fall when the rosehips are in the hedgerows, your rosehip gin will be ready in time for Christmas.

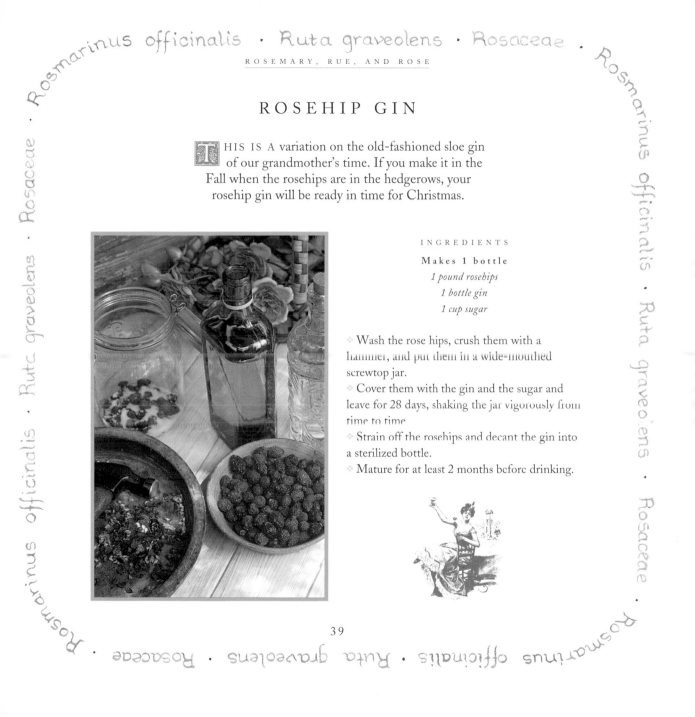

INGREDIENTS

Makes 1 bottle

1 pound rosehips
1 bottle gin
1 cup sugar

❖ Wash the rose hips, crush them with a hammer, and put them in a wide-mouthed screwtop jar.

❖ Cover them with the gin and the sugar and leave for 28 days, shaking the jar vigorously from time to time.

❖ Strain off the rosehips and decant the gin into a sterilized bottle.

❖ Mature for at least 2 months before drinking.

ROSE PETAL JAM

Makes about 4 cups
2 pounds cooking apples
1 pound rose petals
juice of 2 lemons
2 tsps rosewater
2 pounds sugar

TIP
Rose petal jam is delicious spooned over ice cream, rice pudding, or other creamy desserts.

❖ Wash but do not peel the apples, then cut them into chunks. Wash and dry the rose petals, and remove their bitter white "heels."
❖ Put the apples and half of the petals into a large, heavy saucepan, and add water to cover. Cook over medium heat until tender, then stir in the lemon juice.
❖ Strain the mixture through cheesecloth or a jelly bag, without squeezing, until all the liquid is through. Pour the liquid into the pan, add the sugar, the remaining rose petals, and the rosewater, and bring to the boil, stirring constantly. Boil until the liquid reaches 220 degrees on a candy thermometer, or test by dropping a little onto a plate and seeing if it cools to a jelly. Pot into clean Mason jars.

40

ROSE HIP CHUTNEY

INGREDIENTS

Makes about 6 cups

2 medium zucchini

2 tbs salt

1 cup tomatoes

2 medium onions

1 cup rose hips

$2/3$ cup yellow raisins

4 cloves garlic, crushed

$2^{1}/_{2}$ cups light brown sugar

1 tsp ground cinnamon

$^{1}/_{2}$ tsp cayenne pepper

1 tsp ground allspice

2 cups wine vinegar

❧ Chop the zucchini, put them in a colander, sprinkle with salt, and leave for 1 hour to drain.
❧ Meanwhile, skin and chop the tomatoes, and peel and chop the onions.
❧ Crush the rose hips and remove the seeds.
❧ Rinse the zucchini, pat dry, and put in a large heavy pan with the other ingredients.
❧ Heat gently until the sugar dissolves, then cook until the chutney is thick and jelly-like, stirring frequently. Pot into clean jars.

TIP

Rose hip chutney goes well with the soft, mild, spreadable cheeses. Or try it spooned on ham and other similar cold meats in sandwiches or salads.

SCENTED PILLOWS

OTH ROSEMARY and roses retain their scent for a long time when dried, and make delightful scented pillows. Make them on a small scale to tuck behind your head when traveling, to make your journey more comfortable. They are can also be slipped under your pillow at night.

MATERIALS

2 squares fabric the same size
approximately 8 tbs dried potpourri
trimming for the edge
2 cheesecloth squares 1 inch smaller than the
fabric above (optional)

1. Right sides together, sew the two squares of fabric together, leaving a gap for filling. Turn right side out, press. If you are using the cheesecloth as an inner sachet, sew the sides together as above. Fill the sachet with herbs and stitch up the gap in the seam, insert into the cushion and handstitch the gap in the seam. If you are not using a sachet, fill the cushion with potpourri and slipstitch the gap. Sew the trimming in place round the edges to hide the seams.

HUNGARY WATER

H ERBS HAVE BEEN used throughout the ages to make fragrant toilet waters to freshen and scent the body. Flowering tops of rosemary and roses macerated in alcohol are the the basic ingredients of Hungary Water, one of the most ancient perfumes. It was invented in 1370 by a hermit for the 72-year-old Dionna Izabella, the Queen of Hungary, to make "a young face exceedingly beautiful, an old face very tolerable." She claimed that it so improved her health and strength that "on beholding my beauty the King of Poland desired to marry me…"

INGREDIENTS

Makes 3 ³/₄ cups

4 tbs rosemary, preferably flowering tops

4 tbs scented rose petals

4 tbs mint

2 tbs grated lemon rind

1¹/₄ cups rosewater

1¹/₄ cups orangeflower water

1¹/₄ cups vodka

1. Pound the rosemary leaves with the rose petals and mint. Add the grated lemon rind. Transfer to a wide-mouthed jar, and cover with the rosewater, orangeflower water, and vodka.

2. Leave to steep for 2 weeks, then strain into a bottle and seal tightly. Leave to mature for 1 month before using.

44

EAU DE COLOGNE

 AU DE COLOGNE was invented in the 18th century. If you have difficulty in finding bergamot leaves you could use 10 drops of the essential oil instead.

INGREDIENTS

Makes 1½ cups

4 tbs bergamot leaves
8 tbs rosemary leaves
grated rind of 1 orange
grated rind of 1 lemon
3 drops neroli oil
1½ cups vodka

❖ Put all the ingredients in a wide-mouthed jar and cover with the vodka. Leave to macerate for 3 weeks, shaking the jar from time to time.

❖ Strain off into a clean bottle and leave for at least 2 weeks to mature.

COSMETIC CREAMS

BOTH ROSEMARY and rose are essential ingredients for many beauty creams. Rosemary is good for the hair too. Pour boiling water over a handful of rosemary leaves, allow it to cool, strain, and use it as a final rinse. It is best for brunettes as, like sage, it tends to darken the hair. For an extra strong effect, mix rosemary with purple sage. Test it on a lock of hair to check the color before using.

DR GALEN'S COLD CREAM

THIS SIMPLE recipe for cold cream is more than 1800 years old, and was invented by the great physician, Galen, in Greece.

INGREDIENTS

4 tbs olive oil
4 tbs perfumed rose petals
1 tbs beeswax
still spring water

1. Place the oil in a double boiler or in a bowl in the microwave. Heat until it is warm, then pack with rose petals. Cover and leave as long as you can – a minimum of 4 days. Strain.

2. Heat the beeswax, then blend in the perfumed oil and stir until the mixture cools. Beat in enough spring water to give the consistency you need.

ROSE MOISTURE CREAM

TIP

If you are making cosmetic creams in the microwave, err on the side of caution. Process them for just a minute at a time on a low setting.

INGREDIENTS

1 tsp beeswax
1 tsp lanolin
1 tbs almond oil
$^{1}/_{4}$ tsp wheatgerm oil
$^{1}/_{4}$ tsp borax
3 tbs rosewater
6 drops rose oil

❖ Melt the beeswax and the lanolin together with the almond and wheatgerm oils in a double-boiler or in a bowl in the microwave on a low setting.

❖ Dissolve the borax in the rosewater and beat into the mixture.

❖ Stir in the rose oil as it thickens.

TIP

If you don't want to go to the trouble of making your own cosmetic creams, try adding a few drops of essential oil of rose to unscented moisture cream or overnight cream. The easiest way to do this is to just melt the cream on defrost in a microwave, then beat in the rose oil with a fork or a miniature whisk.

ROSE SOAP

MAKING YOUR own soap involves the use of caustic soda which is dangerous to handle. Happily, however, it is possible to make a herb soap of your choice using plain unperfumed bars as a basis. If you want to give your soaps a delicate color, use a few drops of food coloring. Once made, soaps should be left for about a month to harden properly before you use them.

INGREDIENTS

1¼ cups boiling water
1 × 9-ounce bar unperfumed soap
6 drops rose oil

❖ Keep the water on the boil in a saucepan and grate the soap into it, stirring well. Add the rose oil, and continue beating until you have a creamy mix.
❖ Allow the soap to cool, then pour into oiled molds. Or pour it out, knead it, cover with plastic wrap, and roll out. Cut into portions or stamp out shapes with cookie cutters. Leave for 24 hours, then polish with a soft cloth.

ROSEMARY SOAP

THE USE OF oatmeal in this soap makes it a good exfoliater, removing dead surface cells and having an invigorating effect on your skin.

INGREDIENTS

1 cup rosemary leaves
1 × 9-ounce bar unperfumed soap
4 tbs fine raw oatmeal
6 drops rosemary oil

1. Infuse the rosemary in 2½ cups boiling water. Leave for 30 minutes, then strain into a double-boiler. Heat the rosemary water and grate in the soap, stirring occasionally, until the soap has melted.

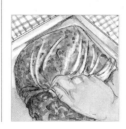

2. Remove from the heat, add the oatmeal and the rosemary oil, and stir. Pour into oiled molds, cover with plastic wrap and roll out. Cut into wedges and leave to harden.

A DRIED ROSEMARY TREE

LITTLE TREES made from dried rosemary make pretty decorations for a shelf, a side-table or on a dining-room table. They can be made from fresh rosemary which is left to dry *in situ*, but dried rosemary twigs are easier to handle and poke into place more firmly. Your tree could be in any one of a number of topiary silhouettes – ball-shaped, conical, or even square.

MATERIALS

terracotta pot
piece of plastic sheeting
plaster of Paris
piece of branch for the tree "trunk"
glue
oasis ball, cone, or square
spaghnum moss
twine or florist's wire
handful of dried rosemary sprigs
about 5 inches long

1. *Line the pot with a piece of plastic. Mix up the plaster of Paris to a thick paste with water and pour it into the pot.*

2. *Before the plaster has set, stick the "trunk" into the pot. When it is firm and the plaster has dried, spread some glue on the top of the trunk and push the oasis onto it.*

3. *Cover the oasis with spaghnum moss, fixing it in place with twine or florist's wire. Push the rosemary sprigs into the moss until the top is completely covered.*

ROSEMARY, RUE, AND ROSE

RICH ROSE POTPOURRI

I N THIS layered potpourri, the scents of the different layers of dried herbs combine with time to give a delicious fragrance. Keep the potpourri for at least six weeks before use. Keeping it well sealed will improve the scent.

INGREDIENTS

2½ cups dried pink and red rose petals
2½ cups dried mint leaves
4 tbs dried rue sprigs
2½ cups dried red rosebuds
4 tbs dried rosemary flowers and leaves
¼ vanilla bean
2 tbs orris root
2 tsp ground cinnamon
½ tsp ground cloves
5 drops rose oil
5 drops rosemary oil
1 drop patchouli oil

1. Put the dried herbs into separate bowls. Chop the vanilla pod finely, mix together with the orris root, cinnamon, and cloves. Mix the oils together in a cup.

2. Put the dried herbs in a wide-mouthed jar in layers, starting with rose petals, then a layer of mint and rue, then rosebuds, and finally the rosemary. On each layer, sprinkle over a little of the orris, cinnamon, and clove mixture, and a drop or two of the oil mixture. Finish with a layer of rose petals.

*They are not long, the
days of wine and roses
Out of a misty dream
Our path emerges for a while, then closes
Within a dream.*
ERNEST DOWSON

HERB CANDLES

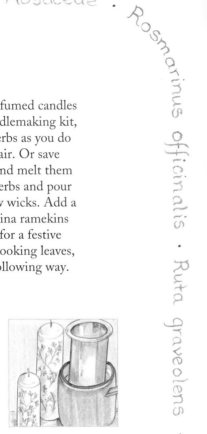

MAKE YOUR own perfumed candles with the aid of a candlemaking kit, stirring in your favorite herbs as you do so, so that they scent the air. Or save leftover pieces of candle and melt them down. Add the chopped herbs and pour them into molds around new wicks. Add a drop of essential oil, and use china ramekins or egg cups to mold floating candles for a festive occasion. Use herbs like rue, with its delicate-looking leaves, to decorate plain or perfumed candles in the following way.

1. Press some sprigs of rue between 2 pieces of kitchen towel or newspaper. Place between the pages of a heavy book, and put several more books on top.

2. When the rue is dry, arrange the sprigs around a large candle. Using the back of a tablespoon that has been heated in boiling water, press the herb gently into place in the wax.

3. Have a double-boiler at the ready, containing clear melted wax. Taking the candle by its wick, dip it quickly and gently into the molten wax until you are sure the rue is covered. Hang the candle up to dry.

ROSEMARY, RUE, AND ROSE

CANDLEMAS
DAY

*In Roman
Catholic
churches, all the
candles which
will be needed
in the church
throughout the
year are
consecrated on
Candlemas Day,
February 2.*

A NEEDLE KEEPER

VICTORIAN needlewomen kept their needles in a little cushion stuffed with dried rosemary leaves. The needle-sharp leaves themselves kept the sewing needles sharpened and free from rust. This charming old custom is due for a revival. The needle-keeper would make a pretty present for anyone who loves needlepoint or embroidery. You could also team the keeper with a matching, rosemary-scented pin-cushion decorated with glass-topped pins. Put a drop or two of essential oil inside with the rosemary leaves to give it an extra fragrance.

MATERIALS

2 diamonds of fabric 5 × 4 inches
2 handfuls well dried rosemary leaves
braid and tassels to trim

❖ With right sides facing, stitch the fabric on 3 sides, leaving a seam allowance of ¹/₂ inch. Stitch in from the corners of the fourth side, leaving a space of at least 2 inches in the center.
❖ Turn the fabric right side out, press it, then fill with dried rosemary until the sachet is plump and firm. Hand-stitch the gap in the seam to close it.
❖ Using a glue gun, or stitching by hand, fix the braid in place to cover the seams, and stitch the tassels in place.

TIP

Use an exotic material from an Indian
shop to make your needle-keeper, or look out for
pieces of extra-wide ribbon instead. Shake your needle-
keeper frequently when filling it, so that the dried
rosemary packs down.

ROSEMARY, RUE, AND ROSE

A ROSE-SCENTED QUILT

IF YOU ARE making a patchwork quilt from scratch, a few small pockets can be incorporated into the design to hold scented rose sachets and help inspire sweet dreams. Alternatively, use a quilt that you already own and sew pockets onto it.

To make a fragrant quilt, choose scraps of fabric which look similar to the ones already incorporated into the quilt. A simple window-design quilt is easy to adapt with square patches of fabric, but different styles of quilt might need to be treated in different ways by adding diamond- or rectangular-shaped pockets. Decide where you wish to place the pockets and where they will fit best into the pattern of the quilt, making sure that they are close to the top end so that you will gain the most benefit from the fragrance.

MATERIALS

scraps of fabric big enough for the pockets
scraps of fabric for appliqué shapes (you could use roses cut out of other fabrics to appliqué onto the pockets)
buttons, ribbons, and embroidery threads as required
fine potpourri
cheesecloth

1. For each pocket, cut a piece of fabric to size to cover the areas chosen for the pocket, adding a ⁵⁄₈-inch seam allowance all around. Make a French seam of ¼ inch then ½ inch on the wrong side along the top of the pocket and slip-stitch it. Turn the seam allowance under on the other 3 sides, tack them in place, and press. Make a buttonhole at the center of the pocket-top if required.

2. Embroider or appliqué fabric shapes onto the pocket, and add simple embroidery stitch detail and small pearl or linen buttons to the pocket to decorate it. Place the pocket in position and slip-stitch along 3 sides leaving the top open. Make a simple cheesecloth sachet to fit inside the pocket and fill it with rose potpourri. Place the sachet in the pocket, and sew a button onto the quilt so that the pocket buttons up and keeps the sachet secure. You could use lengths of ribbon to fasten the pocket-top if you prefer.

INDEX

A

aphrodisiacs 13

B

blisters 17, 22

C

candles 54–5
caramel onions 35
centifolias 19
chicken soup 32
chutney 41
cold cream 46
cooking 32–42
cosmetic creams 46–7

D

damask roses 19
displays 26–7, 30–1
Doctrine of Signatures 10
Dr Galen's cold cream 46
dried rosemary tree 50
drinks 16, 38–9
drying 24–5

E

eau de cologne 45

G

gallicas 19
gin 39

H

hair 46
hair care 46
harvesting 22
hedges 29
herb sachets 43
hips (rose)
    chutney 41
    drying 25
    gin 39
    harvesting 22
Hungary Water 44

J

jam 40

L

lamb 10, 35
layering 20
liqueurs 38
lungwort 10

M

medication 10, 14, 17
moisture cream 47

N

needle-keeper 56

O

onions 35

P

perfumes 13, 18–19, 44, 45
petals (rose)
    drying 25
    harvesting 22
    jam 40
    liqueur 38
    sorbet 36
    syllabub 36
pillows 43
plant care 20–1
potpourri 22, 63
prostrate rosemary 15

Q

quilts 59

R

rosemary 13–15
    caramel onions 35
    chicken soup 32
    cosmetic creams 46
    cushions 43
    dried tree 50
    drying 24
    eau de cologne 45
    hair care 46
    harvesting 22
    hedges 29
    Hungary Water 44
    lamb 10, 35
    needle keeper 56
    plant care 20
    soap 48
    topiary 26–7

S

scrambled eggs 33
seeds 20
soap 48
sorbet 36
soups 32
syllabub 36

T

topiary 26–7

roses 18–19
    cold cream 46
    cosmetic creams 47
    cushions 43
    displays 31
    drying 25
    harvesting 22
    hip chutney 41
    hip gin 39
    Hungary Water 44
    moisture cream 47
    petal jam 40
    petal liqueur 38
    petal sorbet 36
    petal syllabub 36
    plant care 21
    potpourri 53
    quilts 59
    soap 48
rue 16–17
    candles 54
    displays 30
    drying 24
    harvesting 22
    plant care 20
    scrambled eggs 33

ACKNOWLEDGMENTS

The publishers would like to thank
the following companies for their help:

BASKETS AND GLASSWARE
Global Village,
Sparrow Works, Bower Hinton, Martock, Somerset.
Telephone: (01935) 823390

DRIED HERBS AND FLOWERS
The Hop Shop,
Castle Farm, Shoreham, Sevenoaks, Kent TN14 7UB.
Telephone: (01959) 523219

HERB PLANTS BY MAIL ORDER
Jekka's Herb Farm,
Rose Cottage, Shellards Lane, Alveston, Bristol BS12 2SY.
Telephone: (01454) 418878

HERB SEEDS
Suffolk Seeds,
Monks Farm, Pantlings Lane, Coggeshall Road,
Kelvedon, Essex CO5 9PG.
Telephone: (01376) 572456

PICTURE CREDITS
Andrew Lawson Photography; p.28
S & O Matthews Photography: p.21T